Become A Professional Speaker

BUILD YOUR SPEAKING BUSINESS FROM THE GROUND UP

SallyAnn Gray

"WALK IN A ROOM AND CLAIM IT, WALK ON A STAGE AND OWN IT!"

BECOME A PROFESSIONAL SPEAKER MANUAL

Copyright @ 2020. Global Speakers.

All rights reserved. No part of this publication may be reproduced, stored in a retrieval system or transmitted in any form or by any means- electronic, mechanical, photocopying, recording, or any other- except for brief quotations in printed reviews, without the prior permission of the publisher. All scripture quotations are from the Holy Bible, King James or New International Version.

ISBN: 978-1-949343-76-2

Illustrations by Mark Gray
Pictures by Mark Gray
Cover Design by Mark Gray
Edited by SallyAnn Gray
Printed in the United States

Facebook: @globalspeakers
Instagram: @globalspeakerslive
Email: info@globalspeakers.live

THE PROMISE

OBJECTIVES

This manual is designed to:

1. Enhance your technical knowledge and skills in professional speaking.
2. Teach you techniques to keep your audience engaged.
3. Introduce you to the principles of creating a successful speaking career.
4. Get clear on who you should speak to, what you should speak about and get clarity around your speaking topics.
5. Help you deliver a speech that will lead to repeat bookings.

INTRODUCTION

Is a speaker coach really necessary?

We can ask the likes of Les Brown who has spoken openly about seeking mentorship and coaching from the greats who went before him such as Dr. Norman Vincent Peale. Norman Vincent Peale was an American minister and author known for his work in popularizing the concept of positive thinking, especially through his best-selling book The Power of Positive Thinking. I personally consider Les Brown one of the most impactful speakers of all time. If he had a coach to help him achieve the level of impact he has had globally, I think it wise that as speakers we all be coached.

Congratulations on taking this bold step and Congratulations on choosing an intriguing career-path. Half a century ago, it didn't even exist as a paid vocation. Today, it is an entire industry onto itself. Let me take the time to give you your first SPEAKER TIP: you are entering an industry and it is a multi-billion-dollar industry. To get paid in this industry, it requires a keen understanding of what meeting and event planners are looking for when they book a speaker they are willing to pay. Understand that they want to book an expert, and not just a great speaker with an awesome story.

As a speaker, the first thing you must do is shift the focus from you and focus on your target market. The first question you want to ask is who am I speaking to? The second question is, what do they want to hear? What struggles are they facing and how can my speech help them solve their problem? If you think of yourself as a member of the meeting and events industry, or a member of the corporate success industry, you start to look at your target market. You start to consider their needs.

You start to think of this as a career path and a real business solution that you provide.

Professional speaking is an exciting path. Few other careers in the world give you the opportunity to be such an awesome combination of educator, motivator, minister, transformer, entertainer and marketing superstar. It is immensely rewarding, constantly changing, sufficiently challenging to hold your interest, but not so phenomenally difficult as to be unattainable. You can do this. It will take a lot of hard work on your part, but the foundational principles are not difficult to understand and the pathway to success is not a great secret.

Without the right guidance, it is entirely possible for you to float around for years and never really get anywhere. Global Speakers was birthed to ensure this does not happen to you. We know what it means to be passionate about speaking. Speaking is not an option for you, it is a must. So let's get to work! What you will learn here will shorten your learning curve and position you to take steps in the direction that will get you booked, paid and help you make the impact you are desirous of making in the world.

TABLE OF CONTENTS

The Promise iii
    Objectives iii
Introduction v
Chapter 1: Developing The Mindset Of A Professional Speaker 9
    Why? 9
    Who is a Professional Speaker? 9
    What does a Professional Speaker Accomplish? 10
    What is the Mindset of a Professional Speaker? 11
    Profile of a Successful Speaker 11
    What Kind of Speaker am I? 12
    What Problem do I Solve? 12
    What is my Positioning Statement? 13
    My Vision and Mission as a Speaker 13
Chapter 2: Confidently Sharing My Story With Power And Passion 15
    What is my Signature Story? 15
    What do I Hope to Achieve When I Share it? 15
    How will it Shift the Audience to take Action? 15
    How do I Keep my Audience Captivated? 16
    The 5 P's (Probe, Prepare, Practice, Perform, Pray) 18
    The 5 P's for Speaker Success System 18
    Speaker Tip 20
    Opening, Closing and Transitioning Statements 20

Chapter 3: Engaging An Audience For Maximum Impact 21

    How do I Dress for a Speaking Engagement? 21

    How Early do I Arrive? 21

    How do I Engage the Audience Before I Engage them? 21

    How do I Approach the Podium? 22

Chapter 4: Building A Profitable Speaking Business 27

    Establishing your Value in the Marketplace 27

    Establishing a Presence in the Public Domain 28

    Options for Marketing Yourself 28

    Be Awesome Every Time you Speak! 29

    Speak for Free 29

    Write a Book 30

    Develop Products and Programmes 31

    Design a Website to Market Yourself 31

    Maintain a Database 32

    Appear in the Media 32

    Use Social Media 32

    Contact Speaker Agencies 33

    Network with the Right People 33

    Make Direct Contact 33

    Create Special Offers 34

Summary 35

Additional Speaker Resources 37

    Speaker Starter Sheet 39

EXAMPLE OF SPEAKER SHEET 48

CHAPTER 1
DEVELOPING THE MINDSET OF A PROFESSIONAL SPEAKER

WHY?

If you don't have a strong why, it will be hard to ride the tide to your big speaking pay check. Your "WHY" will keep you going in the deepest darkest moments in your life and by extension your speaking career. Why does speaking matter to you? Why does sharing your story matter? Who is counting on you? What truly makes you come alive?

I MUST speak because….

WHO IS A PROFESSIONAL SPEAKER?

- One who is engaged in the profession of public speaking.
- An expert speaker.
- One who speaks for a livelihood on specific topics or subjects.
- One who demonstrates great skill in public speaking.
- A skilled practitioner at public speaking.

- One who gives keynote speeches as a profession.
- One who meets the standards of a professional speaker's association.
- A highly skilled motivational speaker.
- A person whose career is speaking to groups of people.
- One who delivers a public speech for compensation.

The idea of wanting to be a professional speaker, if you have never spoken in front of an audience will not work. The business of public speaking, which has its own intricacies and internal dynamics, is certainly not a 'get-rich-quick' profession. It can be very well paid, indeed, immensely lucrative, but it requires hard work, a high level of speaking skill and the patience necessary to acquire experience. It can take years to earn good money as a speaker.

Step one to becoming a professional speaker, therefore, is learning to speak. The fact that you are consuming information like this programme is a good sign, and I encourage you to consume more such material, but your interest should not be merely academic. If your intention is to make a profession out of speaking, get out there and speak... anywhere and everywhere.

What does a Professional Speaker Accomplish?

Your first practical take-away task from this programme is this: speak, speak, speak. Go and speak anywhere that they will have you. Schools, staff meetings, associations and churches. Take any and every opportunity you can get to rise to your feet and address human beings. At this early stage, your topic will not be as important as getting the speaking practice. Once you have some speaking skills in place, the next thing you will need is a topic (or number of topics) to offer to the market. We will discuss this in Chapter 4.

WHAT IS THE MINDSET OF A PROFESSIONAL SPEAKER?

As a professional speaker, the first thing you must know is you are only as good as your last speech. Understand that the biggest room in the building is the room for improvement. Think of your talks as products that solve a problem rather than just a speech. Why is that important? Our presentations are products that must be sold to buyers, and usually, to companies. The primary thing that we sell is a useful idea that helps people to grow. Don't think of it as a talk. Think of it as a product.

If you have an issue with always wanting to be liked, this will pose a problem. If you have an issue with talking yourself down as a speaker, this will pose a problem. If you cannot handle rejection, this will also pose a problem. You will have to be prepared for people telling you NO for an event you may want to speak at. Your recovery time from the "NO's" in this industry means everything.

To permanently change your effectiveness as a speaker, you must change your self-concept. You must remake yourself. You always perform on the outside in a way that is consistent with your self-concept. All change/improvement in your life begins when you alter and improve your self-concept, your inner programming and your paradigm. What matters most is how you feel about yourself.

PROFILE OF A SUCCESSFUL SPEAKER

- Fearless, confident, high self-esteem.
- Take 100% responsibility for your results as a speaker.
- Intensely goal focused and results oriented.
- Passionate about speaking.
- Strong commitment to adding value to every audience (organization).
- Goes above and beyond the call.
- Has a very pleasing personality. SMILE and SMILE A LOT!
- One who builds relationships. The speaking business is about relationships.

What Kind of Speaker am I?

There are four types of speakers:
- Informational- shares basic information with an audience for the purpose of increasing their knowledge
- Motivational- Pumps an audience up and causes them to want to rise to the occasion and act but does not usually share principles to actually get the task done.
- Inspirational- Shares a great story of insurmountable odds that they overcame. Usually a valley to mountain top story that inspires people so much that they leave the space wanting to act.
- Transformational- The transformational speaker shares in such a way that causes people in the audience to shift thinking and behaviour which usually leads to a more fulfilled life.

What Problem do I Solve?

Your speaking topics are usually birthed out of your pain or biggest struggle. The problem you solve is teaching people how you overcame it.

Reflect on the problem you solve!

WHAT IS MY POSITIONING STATEMENT?

Your positioning statement will stem from the problem you solve.

Example: Hello, I am SallyAnn Gray. I help principals who are frustrated about low staff morale shift the mindset of their staff so they can perform better. Do you believe your teachers may benefit from a mindset shift workshop?

Reflect on your positioning statement!

MY VISION AND MISSION AS A SPEAKER

Your vision as a speaker speaks to where you are going. Your mission says how you plan to do it!

Reflect on your Vision & Mission as Speaker!

Now that you have a good idea of where you are going and how you plan to get there, all you need to do NOW is take that first step.

CHAPTER 2
CONFIDENTLY SHARING MY STORY WITH POWER AND PASSION

WHAT IS MY SIGNATURE STORY?

Your signature story is dependent on what you hope to achieve as a speaker. It also depends on where you plan to go as a speaker or coach. Your story also depends on the needs of your audience. Don't just share a story for sharing it sake. It must go somewhere. You must make a point and make it fast! Your best story is usually tied to your pain, but don't leave your audience in the pain. You must bring them out with a story of overcoming the adversity.

WHAT DO I HOPE TO ACHIEVE WHEN I SHARE IT?

Always ask yourself this, what do I hope to achieve in sharing this story? How will it tie into my speech? Will it help this audience? Am I ok if the world knows this? Don't give more than you are prepared to handle being in the public domain.

HOW WILL IT SHIFT THE AUDIENCE TO TAKE ACTION?

The aim of a GOOD speaker, the aim of a SKILFULL & PASSIONATE speaker is to awaken something in the members of the audience that will cause them to not only feel empowered but take some kind of action on their dreams and goals.

How do I Keep my Audience Captivated?

The first thing to know about keeping an audience captivated is this, speak to issues that affect them. Tell your audience upfront what you will be sharing with them and tie it back to how it will help them. Let the audience know that you are not trying to run their lives, rather you are offering them some tools you have used in your life that caused a shift.

1. Connect with them by sharing from a space of authenticity.
2. Share a story but ensure that it makes a point.
3. Tell a joke.
4. Share a quote that goes somewhere and makes a point.
5. Dress well.
6. Be at ease.
7. Be pleasant.
8. Build suspense and interest stating that you plan to share a really important point.
9. Become an extremely great storyteller. Your audience must sit there and literally feel like they were there as you tell the story. If you give your audience an authentic piece of you, what they will give you in return is their loyalty.
10. Be sensitive to your audience. Know when your speech is not working and be prepared to switch and change the tide.

SallyAnn Gray's
5 Step Speaker Success System

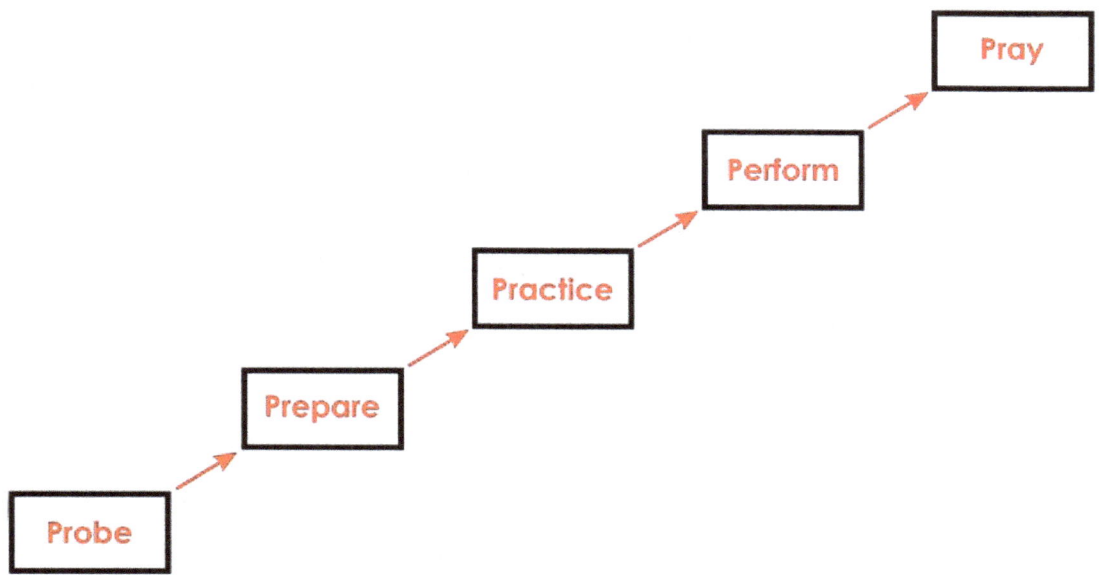

The 5 P's (Probe, Prepare, Practice, Perform, Pray)

<u>The 5 P's for Speaker Success</u> is a system developed by SallyAnn over the past year. Every time she uses it, she leaves an audience with at least 3 requests for another speaking engagement. The event organizer is happy and the audience leaves with a renewed mind and tools for taking action on the issues that affect <u>them</u>.

The 5 P's for Speaker Success System

Probe

Before stepping foot on the stage at an event you must get some pertinent information. Before EVERY speaking presentation I send out a form asking the event organizer to complete. I ask for some information about the organization. Don't just go to an organization or entity and speak on what you feel like speaking on because it is a great speech to you. Every great story is not for every great audience. Speaking is not about how great you are, it's about solving the problem your audience faces (See form on page 47).

Prepare

After the probe comes your preparation. Once you get the form back, use it to craft your message. Never go anywhere with a canned speech, be original every time. Remember, you are only as good as your last speech.

Start with the end in mind. Decide how you want to end the speech, then go back to how you will open. Write your speech by breaking it into parts. The parts are as follows:

- The beginning
- The Middle
- The End

Always start and finish strong. Never tell a sad story at the end. Tell it at the beginning or in the middle so you have an opportunity to bring your audience back up and leave them on a high note.

Decide on 3 to 4 solid points you want to make, then think of a life story that can illustrate that point. Tell a story, share a quote, give an analogy and take the point home. Always make a point and remember your story must tie back into the purpose of your presentation.

Practice

After preparation comes practice. Say your speech aloud to yourself as many chances as you get. Say it in the shower, while getting ready for work. Practice is the key to reducing massive nervousness. Know your speech, know the points you intend to make, know your stories and practice quotes. Practice does not make perfect, practice makes confident. If you feel well prepared and you have practiced your speech it reduces anxiety and you can have more time to focus on engaging with your audience before you actually engage them.

Perform

Find a group of trustworthy and reliable friends. I would say about three. Ensure that at least one of them is also a speaker. The purpose of you performing your speech for them is for to get feedback. They represent your pre-audience. An important tip here, it's important that you get feedback and it is more important that you make the necessary adjustments.

Pray

After you have all you can do in the natural, PRAY and ask God to step in and bring to your remembrance all you have prepared and practiced.

SPEAKER TIP

Record yourself! Every time you speak, ensure it is recorded and watch your own speech. You will recognize that you do things you are simply unaware of during the speech. If you watch yourself, you have an opportunity to observe it and change if necessary.

OPENING, CLOSING AND TRANSITIONING STATEMENTS

Your opening should be engaging and entertaining. A really funny joke, a story, an illustration, an analogy about a great phenomenon of life is always a great way to engage your audience. You literally have three seconds to engage them. Transition properly from one point to the next and ensure points are in a logical sequence. Your close should be very powerful, very strong and it should be a call to action. What are you asking or suggesting the members of the audience do now that you have inspired them?

In summary, once you have decided on the ideas related to the content you will share, it is your responsibility to find ways to make it all come alive, by expressing it through stories, humour, drama, audience interaction, visuals and very clear take-home instructions. When it comes to customization, understand that every audience is different. A presentation should generally comprise around 70% standardized content, and then about 30% customization. A speaker creates additional value by slanting a topic toward the specific audience that will be present on the day. Making it relevant is worth money, and the skill and effort necessary to do that adds to the total value of the presentation.

CHAPTER 3
ENGAGING AN AUDIENCE FOR MAXIMUM IMPACT

How do I Dress for a Speaking Engagement?

Your audience engages with you before you speak. They are looking at how you dress. Does your attire fit the occasion? Are you over dressed? Are you under dressed? Are you comfortably dressed? Your level of comfort can and will impact your presentation. Colors are extremely important, based on the presentation and the point you are trying to make, dress to communicate your posture. Research what colors represent before wearing them. Also, certain colors may cause offence in particular settings.

How Early do I Arrive?

Audiences love real people who are authentic. They like to know you are accessible and you have something in common with them. Star time behavior rarely works especially if you are not yet a star. ARRIVE EARLY! At least 15 minutes before the function starts. If you have a prior engagement and unavoidably arrive right before your speech, address that before you speak so your audience understands why you are late. It makes you human and it makes you likeable. People always want to hear from someone they like!

How do I Engage the Audience Before I Engage them?

Arriving early gives you an opportunity to meet and greet a few people in the audience. Get at least one or two names and try to remember them so you can engage them as you speak. You can refer to them in your speech.

How do I Approach the Podium?

Hug or shake the hand of the person who introduces you. A hug depends on comfort level, culture or the level of relationship you have with the person introducing you. Assume a posture of confidence even if you are not feeling confident. Stand tall and straight with your shoulders back.

SallyAnn Gray's
Triangle Effect For Audience Engagement

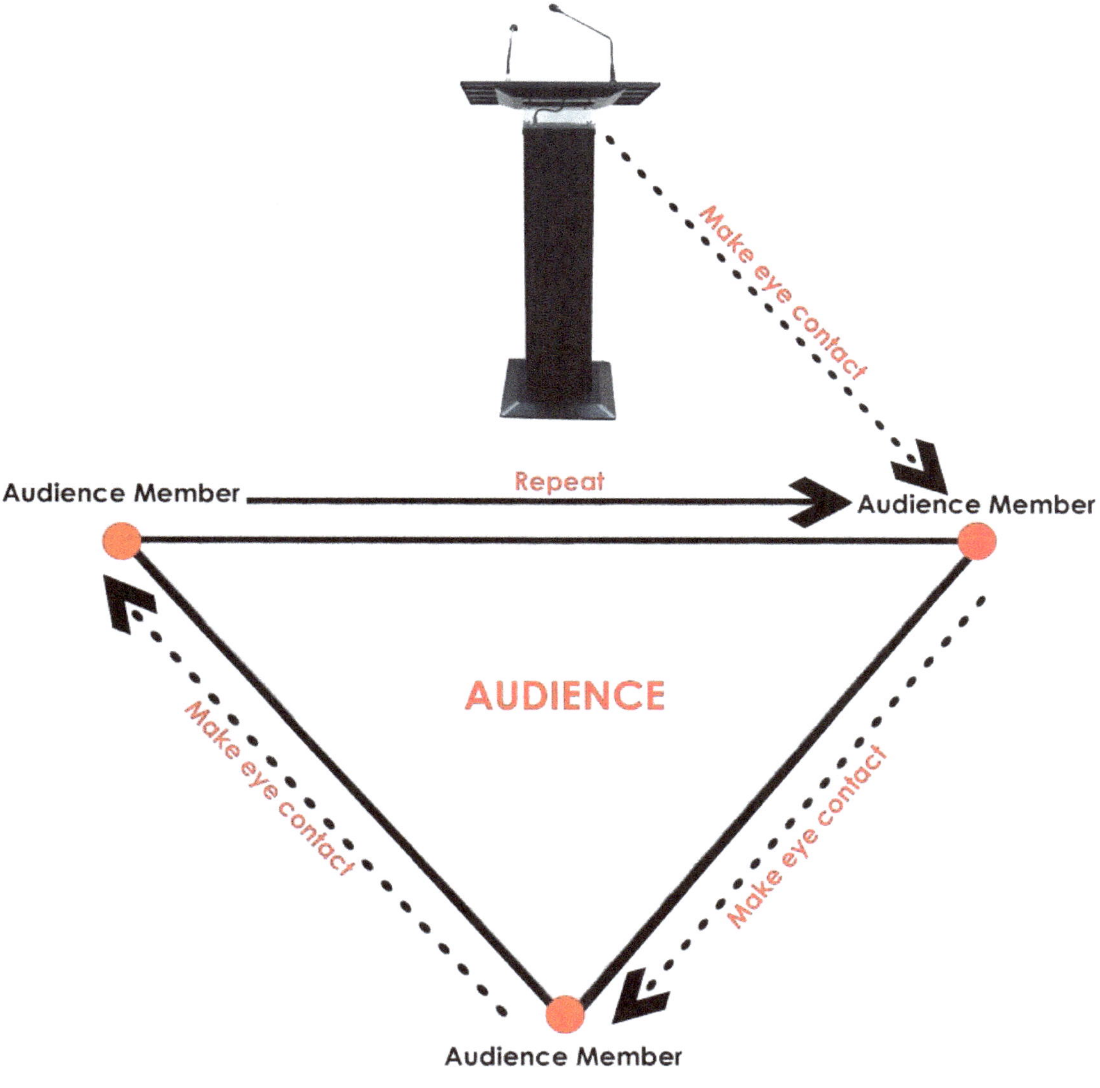

SallyAnn Gray's
6 step
Speech Creation Template

Opening remarks - Acknowledge key stakeholders

Opening - Start with an engaging quote, joke, story, statistic or research findings

---

1st Point

2nd Point

3rd Point

Closing - Start with the end in mind
- Must be powerful
- Must include call to action (what should audience do as a result of what you share?)

SallyAnn Gray's
Point Development Formula

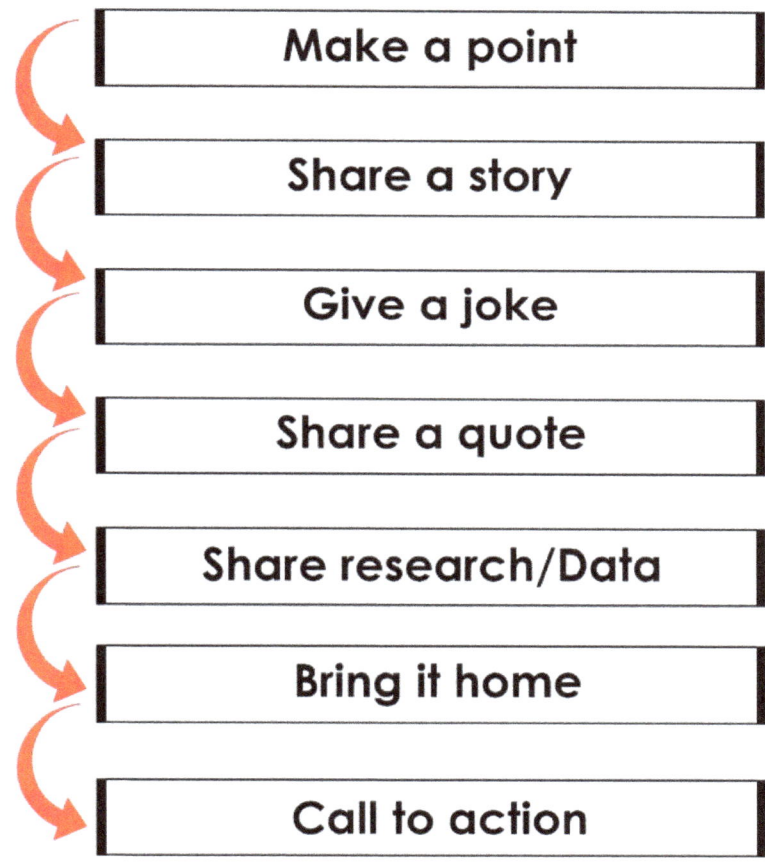

Consider these components as you develop each point within your speech.

CHAPTER 4
BUILDING A PROFITABLE SPEAKING BUSINESS

Establishing your Value in the Marketplace

To make a profession out of speaking, you will need to earn money from it. Unless you speak on a topic that companies or social groups are willing to pay money to hear, you will not earn an adequate income. Provide training, strategy, specialized knowledge, or something of human interest, that is deemed useful or necessary. In other words, you need to provide a product that sells. Your presentation is a product!

Here are some actual topics (products) being used by people who are earning a living as paid speakers:

- Sales
- Leadership
- Mindset
- Communication skills
- Marriage
- Entrepreneurship
- Creating a vision for a company
- Creating a vision for your life
- Time-management
- How to become more productive
- How to Innovate
- How to use both sides of your brain together
- How to live a more balanced life
- How to overcome fear and take chances

- How to become a professional speaker

I believe that my topics all intersect. Essentially, they are about the links between mindset and transformation as a pathway to leading a purposeful and fulfilled life. You could sum up all of my topics using the phrase: Shifting your mindset in order to transform your life! That's my thing. That's what I do. And I make sure that each time I do it, I offer a solid mix of useful ideas and information, humour and entertainment.

Establishing a Presence in the Public Domain

Marketing yourself is the bulk of the work because nobody can book you if they don't know you exist. In fact, you will come to see that 80 percent of your business as a professional speaker, will comprise of marketing yourself.

- You have started honing your speaking skills
- You have developed at least 1 product
- Now you market yourself

Options for Marketing Yourself

If people don't know about you, you can't earn money. If people don't know about you, it doesn't matter how good you are. Get known. Create desire for what you do. That's your primary task in building your career. And you have several different options. Some speakers only do one or two things to build their careers, and become quite successful that way. Some use the full mix. You'll soon see which marketing approaches get the best results for you.

What are the best results? Bookings. Bookings are the goal. Without paying clients who ask you to speak at their events, you don't have a career. Some marketing doesn't lead directly to bookings. It just increases your total visibility. Some increases your credibility, so that when you are being considered for a booking, you come across as a better option than the other speakers who are also being considered.

You can do any mix of the following:
1. Be awesome every time you speak
2. Speak for free
3. Write a book
4. Develop products/programs
5. Maintain a Database (Lead List)
6. Appear in the media
7. Use social media
8. Become a member of a Speakers Bureau
9. Network with the right people
10. Make direct contact (with meeting planners & event organizers)
11. Create special offers (win a book/speech/give something free)

BE AWESOME EVERY TIME YOU SPEAK!

There is no better way to promote you quite as effectively as you, in action, being really awesome! It doesn't happen often in the early stages of a speaker's career, but as you get better and better at your stage-craft, your entertainment- factor, your engagement with the audience; the total brilliance of what you do; you will start finding that speeches generate more speeches.

SPEAK FOR FREE

I recommend this to every speaker who truly wants to launch a career. It's called paying your dues, but it's not a punishment. It's a very clever and effective way of building a career. Speak for free for anyone who will have you around: schools, businesses and social clubs. The objective is twofold: to practice, and to become known. Your speeches are your greatest marketing tool. My biggest source of revenue is repeat bookings and referrals. Always ask for referrals.

The most important thing is to capture every speech. Get a professional videographer to record your presentation. Video footage of yourself in action is very, very important to you. This is your single most important marketing tool. If you have a good number of speech clips available to view online, this alone, increases your credibility. Videos matter greatly. Get as much of it as you can. The higher the quality, the better for you!

WRITE A BOOK

Writing a book establishes you as an expert on a particular subject. Meeting planner's book and pay experts. Nothing increases your credibility, or visibility, quite like having a book in print. It does not matter that it is not a New York Times bestseller. Publish a book and you are regarded as an authority.

Another advantage of publishing a book is that you can use it to gain publicity. You can be interviewed for television or radio talk-shows. There are many things you can do to enhance your marketing efforts with a book behind your name. Some speakers' agents urge their clients to consider self-publishing instead of submitting their manuscript to a publisher. Their rationale is that potentially you can make more money by selling your own books after your presentations than by having them on the shelf in bookstores, where you profit per book is less.

The other side of the coin is that a publisher can achieve greater reach for you by retailing your books. And there is an element of satisfaction to having your book 'accepted' rather than simply paying for its publication yourself. Being accepted by a publisher carries much greater credibility and total clout. Eventually, you will want to go this route. I've done both. Writing a book is an excellent way to boost your speaking career, and although the profit margins from book sales are not generally very high initially, they do add an additional income stream to your total revenue.

DEVELOP PRODUCTS AND PROGRAMMES

As a speaker, the number of products you can develop and sell is limited only by your imagination and willingness to put in the work. The great thing about products is that once they are developed, and once you've paid to have them produced, the profits grow exponentially. Develop one audio CD, and you'll always have one to sell. Increase it to three, and you will always have three items selling, and so on.

Here is a list of some options for products that you can develop to increase your total professional presence and expertise:

- Books
- DVD's
- DVD Sets
- CD's
- CD sets
- Audio books
- Online blogs
- Speeches
- Workshops
- Seminars and bootcamps
- Workbooks, which allow the buyer to answer questions directly within the product
- E-courses
- Newsletters
- Downloadable MP3 guides

DESIGN A WEBSITE TO MARKET YOURSELF

You can't be a professional speaker without a website. Use your website to show the value you offer. Demonstrating real value is the only way to have a sustained career in this industry. Branding and marketing materials help: websites, business cards, brochures, banners, books, and so on, all help to elevate you from 'someone who is trying to be a speaker,' to someone who is serious. Impression is EVERYTHING!

Maintain a Database

Most speakers collect contact details in order to create and grow a database of names, to which they send out newsletters and make offers. I am currently developing myself in this area. It is a great way to earn, increase visibility and develop your tribe.

Appear in the Media

If you have a book it will be easy to get a TV appearance. Professional speakers appear in the media quite frequently. Sometimes they will even become a journalist's 'go to' source for commentary on a given issue.

The key, is the value that you can add to a program. For example, if it is the beginning of a new year, you can contact several talk-show hosts and offer to speak on the topic of motivation for their listeners as they begin their new year. How to set goals, How to maintain a growth mindset etc.

Use Social Media

Be available online. I'm on YouTube, LinkedIn, Instagram & Facebook. I am constantly announcing to the world, whether it's simple motivational quotations or links to new video clips that I am here. May I suggest a YouTube account. The more video footage you have available online, the better for your growing professional speaking career.

One important thing to remember when uploading your videos, platforms like YouTube allow you to add key words or phrases to your video. In addition to keywords that describe the content in my videos, I add the terms: professional speaker, motivational speaker, conference speaker, keynote speaker, inspirational speaker, and so on. The whole point in uploading these videos is to make it easier for potential clients to find you.

Contact Speaker Agencies

Network with speaker agencies. They can help add credibility to your portfolio. Not all are credible, and some are flat out a waste of time. The right one will help you get speaking gigs that align with your brand. Partnering with a great speaker agency may account for about 40% of total speaking gigs. When you target speaker agencies and bureaus, you need to have a number of speeches under your belt before an agency will consider representing you. Not all agencies are about mentoring or growing new speakers. You will also need to have clarity on your subject matter and target audience. If you don't know what you sell, and to whom, how can they possibly sell you any more effectively?

Network with the Right People

Every social function provides some opportunity for networking. Have business cards ready, be prepared to actively promote yourself, and consider investing in a book on how to develop networking skills. Make it a point of duty to network with other speakers. Why? Because speakers can't always handle all the engagements that come their way. And if they know, like and trust you, they will share business with you by recommending you for an engagement they are unable to execute on.

Make Direct Contact

Write directly to meeting planners, event organizers, the director of a division, the CEO of an organization, the head of regional sales, or it could be training or events companies. Offer your services and have a nicely written biography along with a link to your website to send to them.

It is a time-consuming task but yields great rewards. Always ensure that you are speaking to the right person. Speak to the person who owns the problem you provide a solution to. The person who feels their emotional effect in his or her everyday business life. Be sure to talk about 'what they can get' from booking you, rather than just 'who you are'. Your fees are largely based on 'what they can get.' It means the difference between a headline such as: 'Sally the Fantastic Speaker!' and 'Is a poor mindset affecting the effectiveness of your teachers? Let SallyAnn Gray help shift their mindset so they can increase overall effectiveness! The latter is benefit orientated, solves an emotional problem, and will meet with greater success.

The more you try, the greater your chances of success. Two letters will simply not be enough. You need to send out hundreds.

Create Special Offers

People like free, so offer something for free to them. Could you create a special offer? Win a book, win a speech, something along those lines? With a little strategic thought, you can use this avenue to publicize your offerings.

SUMMARY

So what makes a speech valuable? It is more than a great smile! Here are a few:

- Solving a Problem
- Knowledge in a subject matter
- Great storyteller
- Celebrity Status
- Credentials
- Entertainment value
- Humor

Ever heard of the speaker who is all flash and mouth with no substance? They're not generally spoken of in glowing terms and not necessarily re-booked but there is value in flash. Entertainment is worth money. People will pay for good clean energy. Naturally, the key is to balance flash with substance, showmanship with good solid content, entertainment value with useful and applicable knowledge. These are usually the hallmark of a great speaker, and this my friend, is how you get paid!

How do I charge is the biggest question I get from emerging speakers. My answer is this, charge based on the value you know you bring to the needs of an organization. Of course, there are two values at play here. The value you ascribe to yourself and the value you are perceived as having. The value event organizers are willing to pay is based on accrued value. You will only develop this over time. Like any other industry, you have to pay your dues.

If you offer value, people will pay you respect and give you what is due.

ADDITIONAL SPEAKER RESOURCES

Speaker Starter Sheet

What vision do I have for myself as a speaker?

_____

_____

_____

_____

What is my mission?

_____

_____

_____

_____

What is my income goal?

_____

_____

_____

What do people come to me most about?

_____

_____

_____

_____

Ideally who would I speak to in an audience?

_____

_____

_____

_____

What resources can I produce in my area of expertise?

_____

_____

_____

_____

_____

What value do I bring to the needs of an organization?

_____

_____

_____

_____

Do I already have any speaking experience?

_____

_____

_____

_____

Do I have high quality footage of my speaking engagements?

_____

_____

_____

_____

What social media platforms will I use to market my services?

_____

_____

_____

_____

Do I have a website?

_____

_____

_____

_____

Do I already have some contacts to leverage my connections for more speaking engagements?

_____

_____

_____

_____

What products will I use to establish myself as an authority?

_____

_____

_____

_____

SallyAnn Gray

SPEAKING CAREER
Starter Pack

SPEAK NOW!

- ✓ Mindset of a speaker
- ✓ An identified speaker you will understudy
- ✓ Vision Statement
- ✓ Mission Statement
- ✓ Business Name
- ✓ Problem you solve
- ✓ Speaking Topics
- ✓ Speaker One Sheet
- ✓ Speaker Reel (professional video footage)
- ✓ At least 2 speaking gigs under belt
- ✓ Social media handles
- ✓ Content for posts (quotes, pictures, videos)
- ✓ Business Cards
- ✓ Professional Pictures
- ✓ Website

www.globalspeakers.live | info@globalspeakers.live | @globalspeakers

SallyAnn Gray

Create this document in google forms and send the link to event planners

YOUR LOGO AND LETTER HEAD
Event Needs Assessment Form

We ask that this information be completed and sent via email at least 7 days prior to the event.

Organization/Company Name:

Date:

Start Time:

End time:

Possible # of Attendees:

Theme of event:

Speaker Topic:

1. Who will attend?
2. Indicate the names and titles of leaders within the organization the speaker must acknowledge in opening remarks.
3. What demographic will make up the audience? Tick the one that applies.

Men only: _____

Women only: _____

Both: _____

Children: _____ (Maybe a few Girls)

4. What is the average age of the audience?

___

5. What is the education level of the audience?

___

6. What frustrations do they experience as they provide services to your organization?

___
___

7. What are the sensitive issues? Are there controversial issues that should be avoided?

___
___
___

8. What is the biggest challenge your company/group is facing today?

___
___

9. What are the strategic goals of the organization?

___
___
___

10. What other information might be helpful for the speaker to know?

_____
_____

11. How do you want your people, students, servicemen/women to feel when they leave the speaker's presentation?

_____
_____

12. How did you hear about SallyAnn Gray?

_____

EXAMPLE OF SPEAKER SHEET

"Shifting Mindsets Tranforming Lives"

RELEVANT. RELATIONAL. RIVETING

SallyAnn Gray is a professional member of the National Speakers Association. As an award-winning Author, Educational Consultant, Special Education Trained Teacher, Entrepreneur, International Speaker, Public Speaking Trainer, Wife and Mother, SallyAnn does it all! How? By being intentional about saying NO to the things that do not align with her core mission in life.

She has engaged thousands of teachers, teenagers, parents and corporate groups in high impact speeches, workshops and seminars and is one of the most requested speakers in Jamaica. She holds a Master's degree in Educational Leadership from Virginia Commonwealth University and has a Bachelor's degree in Special Education from the University of the West Indies. SallyAnn was nominated and won the Indie Legacy Author of the Year Award, for her first book, The Renewal: Revive Everything Necessary Empower Within. An honour she received in Baltimore, Maryland in June 2019.

At just 20 years old, SallyAnn was awarded the Jamaica Association of the Deaf Shield, for best performance in Education, upon her graduation from the Mico University College. SallyAnn has taught in Jamaica & the United States. She boasts a flourishing career as an educational consultant, where she focuses on the development of teachers, teenagers and parents, by finding solutions to social problems. SallyAnn's mission is to shift the mindset of teenagers globally, so they can transform their own lives. She has recognized in her work, that in order to develop youth, she must also focus on positive parenting. Her most recent book, 'Wayward Teen to Transformed Queen: Strategies to Help your Teenager Succeed' is a manual for parents of teenagers.

SallyAnn has written curriculum for the National Training Agency of Jamaica and is also a school inspector with the National Education Inspectorate of Jamaica. In her last professional role, she was Head of School & Programs Director for the TGL School of Sales & Sales Management.

SallyAnn is the founder of Global Speakers, an organization dedicated to training and developing emerging speakers to create global impact, using the power of their story. Given away by her mother at three months old, diagnosed with Attention Deficit Hyperactivity Disorder (ADHD) at fifteen years old and kicked out of high school at the age of seventeen, SallyAnn is no stranger to adversity. Her mantra is this "Anything is possible for him who believes, I don't think limits!"

Her Philosophy is simple

"I REMAIN COMMITTED TO GROWTH IN ALL AREAS OF MY LIFE. WHEN I GROW, I GROW OTHERS."

WWW.SALLYANNGRAYSPEAKS.COM

SALLY'S SIGNATURE PRESENTATIONS

MINDSET MASTERY THAT MOVES MOUNTAINS

Format: 60-90-minute keynote (Can be customized)

This program is perfect for:
- Corporate teams who require a productivity boost and inspiration
- Associations required to fulfil a huge mandate
- School administrators & teachers at the beginning of a School Year or a new term

GET ROOTED! GET PLANTED! GET GOING!

Format: 60 minute keynote (Can be customized)

This program is perfect for:
- Teenage boys & girls in school settings
- Teenage boys & girls at youth retreats & youth conferences
- At Risk Youth in Juvenile, Detention & Remand Center

LOVE, LEARN, TEACH & INCREASE

Format: 2-hour keynote/seminar/breakout session (Can be customized)

This program is perfect for:
- General Education Teachers in Secondary Institutions
- Special Education Teachers in Secondary Institutions
- Student teachers (Education Preparation Programs at the Secondary Level)

THE POWER OF POSITIVE PARENTING

Format: 60-90-minute keynote (Can be customized)

This program is perfect for:
- Parents of Teenagers
- Parents of At-Risk-Youth
- Knowledge of how to create and execute on the Individualized Success Plan (ISP)

For additional information on these programs please peruse SallyAnn's NSA profile by clicking the logo below:

WWW.SALLYANNGRAYSPEAKS.COM

AREAS OF EXPERTISE

SALLYANN SPEAKS ON

MINDSET RENEWAL IN THE AREAS OF:

1. **PERSONAL DEVELOPMENT**
2. **PARENTING**
3. **PURPOSE**
4. **PUBLIC SPEAKING**

Sally's only reason for speaking, training and teaching people, is to stimulate and develop human potential. She delivers relevant, relational and riveting messages that fosters a shift in mindset. She creates and delivers keynote presentations and workshops to teachers, parents, teenagers and corporate groups, equipping them to leave mediocrity behind and step into excellence.

What's the best way to get started with your mindset revolution? One way is to identify where you may have fixed tendencies so that you can work to become more growth minded. We all live on a continuum, and consistent self-assessment helps us become the person we want to be.

Mindset renewal is an inquiry into the power of our beliefs, both conscious and unconscious, and how changing even the simplest of them can have profound impact on nearly every aspect of our lives. A "fixed mindset" assumes that our character, intelligence, and creative ability are static givens which we can't change in any meaningful way. A "growth mindset," on the other hand, thrives on challenge and sees failure not as evidence of unintelligence but as a heartening springboard for growth and for stretching our existing abilities. Out of these two mindsets, which we manifest from a very early age, springs a great deal of our behaviour, our relationship with success and failure in both professional and personal contexts, and ultimately our capacity to lead fulfilled lives.

Begin your journey of growth today.

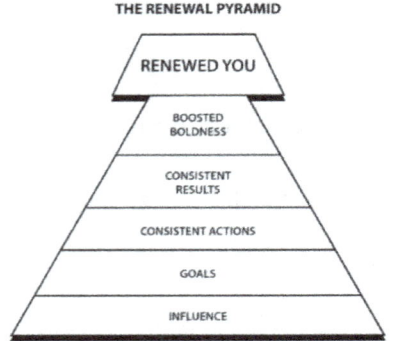

Diagram by SallyAnn Gray. Excerpt from 'The Renewal'

WWW.SALLYANNGRAYSPEAKS.COM

GLOBALLY REQUESTED SPEAKER

From international conference stages to schools, churches and corporate companies, SallyAnn creates customized presentations that meets the needs of an audience. An effective communicator and curriculum designer, SallyAnn crafts presentations that speaks to the bottom-line strategic objectives of organizations. She delivers the presentation in such a way, that it shifts the mindset of the audience. Whether she speaks to corporate groups, teachers, parents or teenagers, the result is the same 'A SHIFT IN MINDSET' which will transform lives.

SallyAnn is one of the most requested speakers in Jamaica and has delivered keynote presentations to government agencies, corporate entities and schools across the island.

BOOK SALLYANN TO SPEAK!

info@sallyanngrayspeaks.com

+1 876-838-8440 Makeda Laylor, Manager

Her most popular keynotes are:

- POSITIVE PARENTING:
  STRATEGIES TO HELP YOUR TEEN SUCCEED

- THE POWER OF A TRANSFORMED MIND:
  TIPS FOR CREATING A GROWTH MINDSET

- CHANGE YOUR STORY, CHANGE YOUR LIFE
  THE MESSAGE OF YOU, HOW TO CREATE GLOBAL IMPACT

WWW.SALLYANNGRAYSPEAKS.COM

A poor mindset will rob anyone of the life they deserve!

In her debut book, SallyAnn bravely shares how being adopted and diagnosed with ADHD caused her to develop a poor mindset. Her poor mindset plagued her during much of her adult life, despite external success. In this honest self-reflection of her most stressful moments, SallyAnn chronicles the steps she has taken to shift her mindset.

SallyAnn now thrives on a growth mindset and has developed a formula for daily mind renewal. She offers this formula to executives, teachers, parents and teenagers to stop the self-sabotage and embrace who they have been called to be.

SALLYANN GRAY HELPS PARENTS TO SHIFT THEIR MINDSET ON PARENTING

"When its all said and done, as parents, we all want well rounded, well adjusted contributing members of society as our offspring. In the end, it won't matter so much what their profession is: lawyer, doctor, Indian or chief. What will matter most is WHO they are." Whether you believe it or not parents, whether you embrace it or not, we have a HUGE role to play in that. Let us lead them not only in words but in deeds. For what we do will have a much bigger impact than what we say."

-Excerpt, Wayward Teen to Transformed Queen: Strategies to Help your Teenager Succeed

ARE YOU PLANTED IN PURPOSE? SALLYANN WILL SHIFT YOUR MINDSET WHEN IT COMES TO PURPOSE!

Many in fact do start, but what does it take to remain consistent and finish your course? How do you remain rooted when life knocks you down? Is there a way to keep your focus despite the worries of life? Are the limits we see even real or are they self-imposed bars?

WWW.SALLYANNGRAYSPEAKS.COM

GOVERNMENT AGENCIES THAT HAVE WORKED WITH SALLY

SCHOOLS & UNIVERSITIES THAT HAVE WORKED WITH SALLY

COMPANIES THAT HAVE WORKED WITH SALLY

SALLY IN THE MEDIA

SALLYANN GRAY IS 'SHIFTING MINDSETS & TRANSFORMING MINDS'

SALLYANN HELPS OTHERS GET 'PLANTED IN PURPOSE'

TVJ INTERVIEW- SALLYANN HELPS OTHERS TO SHIFT THEIR MINDSET WITH THE POWER OF HER STORY

SALLYANN GRAY ENCOURAGES TEENAGERS TO READ AS A PATHWAY TO SHIFTING THEIR MINDSET

CVM AT SUNRISE TV INTERVIEW WITH SALLYANN GRAY

INSPIRE ME THE POWER OF A CHANGED MIND

WHAT PEOPLE HAVE TO SAY

In just one moment with SallyAnn Gray, she inspired and invigorated my spirit! It is like oxygen to hear from her as she breathes words of encouragement to uplift me on this journey of life. She served as a panelist at my Premium Business Networking Signature Forum and she did not disappoint. Every person in the room left feeling inspired and empowered to take some serious action in their own life. The tips she shared on developing a growth mindset are practical and gave members of the audience great insight on how to make some immediate changes. We are looking forward to working with her again.

Erica McKenzie,
President & CEO, Creative Brands & Concepts- Jamaica

From the moment she opened her mouth, SallyAnn riveted the audience with her sense of humor. Her speech was impactful to say the least. She gave us practical tools we could implement immediately to develop a growth mindset. SallyAnn is a dynamic speaker and has the ability to help audiences dig deeper as they look for greater achievement in their careers and lives.

Paul Bryan,
Managing Director, Think Grow Lead-Training Masters

This lady needs no introduction, I am positive she will change the world with her powerful story. She was funny, witty, informative, inspiring and empowering. The questions SallyAnn asked the audience as she delivered her presentation caused us to pause, think and become reflective to the deeper calling we all have as human beings. Without hesitation, I highly recommend SallyAnn to any conference organizer seeking to inspire their audience to pursue greatness.

Jill Primm,
Founder, Restore Women's Conference- California

SallyAnn isn't your typical keynote speaker!
With her dynamic and interactive style,
she moves her audience into action by
giving strategies to renew their mind and create bottom line results!

WHY HIRE SALLY?
SallyAnn will partner with you to achieve the objectives of your event.
She has two main goals:
1) Make YOU, the event planner SHINE!
2) Give your attendees powerful
and practical content they can
take action on NOW!

Speaker Notes

Speaker Notes

Speaker Notes

SPEAKER NOTES

SPEAKER NOTES

SPEAKER NOTES

SPEAKER NOTES

SPEAKER NOTES

Speaker Notes

Speaker Notes

Speaker Notes

www.ingramcontent.com/pod-product-compliance
Lightning Source LLC
Chambersburg PA
CBHW081755100526
44592CB00015B/2449